# English Code 3

## Grammar Book

# Contents

# Welcome!

**1** 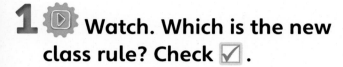 **Watch. Which is the new class rule? Check ☑ .**

Never forget your pencil. ☐

Always come to school early. ☐

Don't bring rabbits to class. ☐

Answer the teacher's questions. ☐

**2** 🔘 **Read and match. Watch to check.**

1  Raise ●—          ● a  your books.

2  Don't bring ●—     ● b  to each other.

3  Don't ●—           ● c  your hand to speak.

4  Always remember ●— ● d  rabbits to class.

5  Listen ●—          ● e  be late.

**3** **Read and check ☑ the right class rules. Correct the wrong ones.**

## CODE CRACKER ⚙️⚙️⚙️

1  Don't listen to the teacher. ☐ _____

2  Eat in class. ☐ _____

3  Have fun. ☐ _____

4  Ask a question when you don't understand. ☐ _____

5  Don't work hard. ☐ _____

# Language lab

*I will talk about classroom rules.*

**1** Look at the picture and read the story. What is different about school on Planet Strange? Check ☑.

a   There aren't any teachers.   ☐

b   The students can do what they like.   ☐

### In class on Planet Strange

Everything's different on Planet Strange. The students don't have class rules. Look at the students and the things they do. Xadu doesn't walk in class, he runs! CooKoo draws on the board. Zaz closes the door very hard. Soomi writes in a library book, and Wiggle eats his lunch in class. The teacher is Mr. Moog. "What good students!" he says. Then the students from Planet Strange travel to Earth. "School's different on Planet Earth," says Mr. Moog. "There are new classroom rules to learn!"

**2** The students learn new rules. Match the rules to the students' names.

### Rules

① Don't eat in class. ●

② Don't draw on the board. ●

③ Walk in the classroom. Don't run! ●

④ Close the door quietly. ●

⑤ Don't write in the library books. ●

● Xadu

● Wiggle

● Zaz

● CooKoo

● Soomi

**3** Read the rules again. Underline the action words and don't in the rules.

# 4 Circle the correct word.

1 **Draw** / **Don't draw** on the wall.

2 **Read** / **Don't read** comics in class.

3 **Listen** / **Don't listen** to the teacher.

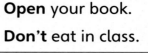

**Open** your book.
**Don't** eat in class.

# 5 Look at the sentences. Which sentence is a rule, a or b? Circle. What is different about the rules?

1 a  Jane doesn't eat in the classroom.    b  Don't eat in the classroom.

2 a  Listen to the teacher.    b  I listen to the teacher.

# 6 Look, read, and complete.    draw  sing  speak  write

1 _____ with the children.

2 _____ on the board.

3 _____ with a pencil.

4 _____ when the teacher speaks.

# 7 Write four rules for your classroom. Use rules from 2 to help you.

Don't eat a sandwich in class.

# 1 Show time!

**1**  **Watch. What is Freddie doing? Check ☑.**

acting ☐    doing gymnastics ☐

juggling ☐    eating carrots ☐

**2** **Read and circle. Watch to check.**

1   They ( are ) / is  practicing for the show.

2   What  are / ( is )  Yara doing?

3   What ( are ) / is  you doing?

4   I'm  do / ( doing )  gymnastics.

5   She isn't  practice / ( practicing )  for the show.

**3** **Do a class survey. Record your results in a bar graph.**

**CODE CRACKER**

**What are you doing at the Talent Show?**

juggling    acting    doing gymnastics

**Results**

_____ students are juggling.

_____

_____

_____

# Language lab 1

WHAT ARE YOU / HE / SHE / THEY DOING?

> I will talk about actions using **be** and **-ing**.

## 1 Read. Which sentence matches the story best? Check ☑.

1   Alice is juggling at the school show and Andy is dancing.  ☐

2   Andy and Alice are playing the trumpet at the school show.  ☐

3   Alice and Andy are performing in the school show and they're great.  ☐

### Talented Alice and Andy

Alice and Andy have many talents. What are they doing today? They aren't reading a book at home. They're performing in the school show and they're great!

Look at Andy. He's playing the trumpet and he's dancing. He's great with music!

What is Alice doing? Is she juggling? No, she isn't. And she isn't doing cartwheels. She's also in the school show. She's singing and helping at the show!

Now the show is over and Alice and Andy are waving. People are clapping!

trumpet

## 2 Read again. Order the events.

He's playing a trumpet.  ☐

People are clapping!  ☐

They're performing in the school show.  ☐

She's helping at the show.  ☐

Alice and Andy are waving.  ☐

**What are you doing?**
I'm juggling. I'm not singing.

**What's he doing?**
He's waving. He isn't acting.

**Are they stamping?**
Yes, they are. / No, they aren't.

## 3 Read again. Underline the words that end in -ing.

# 4 Circle the correct word.

1 The cat's ( play / playing ) with a ball in the living room.

2 I ( am reading / aren't reading ) a story in English!

3 ( Am / Is ) Joanna doing magic tricks? Yes, ( she is / she isn't ) .

4 They ( aren't spinning / isn't spinning ) around.

5 What ( are / is ) Adam doing? He's doing his homework.

# 5 Put the words in order.

1 ( jumping ) ( am ) ( I )

_____.

2 ( the children ) ( reading ) ( are )

_____.

3 ( singing ) ( isn't ) ( Harry )

_____.

# 6 Complete the sentences with the correct form of the action words.

do   practice   spin   step

1 Oscar and Alex _____ for the show. ☑

2 Tess _____ backward. ☑

3 I _____ cartwheels. ☒

4 _____ they _____ around? ☑

**Watch out!**

clap = clapping

# 7 🗨 Mime an action. Ask a partner to say what you are doing.

What am I doing?

Are you dancing?

Yes, I am!

# Language lab 2

DESCRIBING ACTIONS

> I will describe actions using **well / quickly / badly**.

## 1 Read. Circle the words that describe the actions.

Hey! All the children are practicing for the show. Brad is doing cartwheels well. And there are Ben and Emma! They're doing gymnastics carefully. Oh, no ... Listen to Jake! He's singing really loudly! And look at me! I'm spinning around quickly.

## 2 Circle the correct word.

1 My sister is playing the piano badly / bad .

2 She's running very slow / slowly .

3 Katia and Ruth are dancing really beautifully / beautiful .

4 He's talking quietly / quiet .

5 I'm reading good / well .

| Describing things | Describing actions |
|---|---|
| bad | I'm juggling **badly**. |
| quiet | You're reading **quietly**. |
| loud | They're stamping **loudly**. |
| good | We're acting **well**. |
| careful | They're doing gymnastics **carefully**. |

## 3 Complete the sentences with the correct form of the words.

1 You are spinning around _____ (quick).

2 Eva and Mark are acting _____ (good).

3 They are stamping _____ (loud).

4 He's juggling _____ (careful).

9

# 2 Frozen

## 1 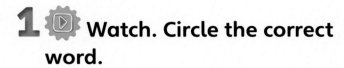 Watch. Circle the correct word.

1 Mammoths / Elephants were from the Ice Age.

2 Mammoths were icy / hairy .

3 Mammoths weren't a type of dinosaur / elephant .

## 2 Read and complete. Watch to check.

was (2)   wasn't   were (2)   weren't

1 Where were you, Ellie? I _____ outside.

2 Mammoths _____ the same as elephants – they _____ hairy.

3 Was it rainy? No, it _____ . It _____ snowy.

4 _____ there dinosaurs in the Ice Age?

## 3 Look and label the categories. Add your own ideas to each category.

### CODE CRACKER

| 1 _____ | 2 _____ |
|---|---|
| elephants, rabbits, warm and sunny, _____ _____ | mammoths, rabbits, cold and icy, _____ _____ |

# Language lab 1

IT WAS / WAS NOT ...

> I will talk about the past.

## 1 Look at the picture and read. How old is Lily now? Check ☑.

three ☐     eight ☐     65 ☐

My name is Lily. This is a picture of me with my grandma and grandpa. We were outside the Natural History Museum. It was warm and sunny. We were very happy. In the picture I was three. Now I'm eight.

When I visit my grandparents, I have a great time! We look at pictures of dinosaurs. They tell me things. In the past, my grandma was a science teacher. "Were you a good teacher?" I ask. "Yes, I was!" she answers. "I was a very good teacher."

My grandpa wasn't a teacher. He was an actor. He doesn't act now. He's 65. He likes music.

I like to think about the past. My grandma and grandpa weren't always old. My grandma was a little girl. My grandpa was a little boy.

## 2 Read again. Complete the sentences.

1 Lily was _____ the Natural History Museum in the picture.

2 Lily's grandmother was a
_____ .

3 Lily's grandfather was an
_____ .

I **was** a teacher. I **wasn't** an actor.

He **was** happy. He **wasn't** sad.

You **were** sad. You **weren't** happy.

**Was** she a good teacher?
Yes, she **was**. / No, she **wasn't**.

**Were** they young?
Yes, they **were**. / No, they **weren't**.

## 3 Read again. Underline was, wasn't, were, and weren't.

# 4 Circle the correct answer for you.

1 Were you at school yesterday?            Yes, I was. / No, I wasn't.
2 Was your grandpa a teacher?             Yes, he was. / No, he wasn't.
3 Was it hot last week?                   Yes, it was. / No, it wasn't.
4 Was it Thursday yesterday?              Yes, it was. / No, it wasn't.
5 Were you happy yesterday?               Yes, we were. / No, we weren't.

# 5 Read and match the words to the correct category.

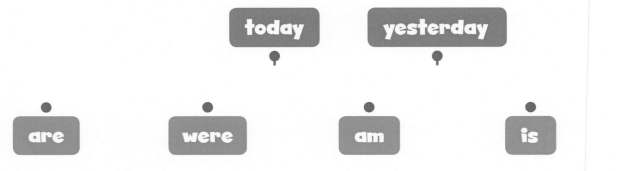

today    yesterday

are    were    am    is    was

# 6 Complete the sentences with the words from the box.

are   is   was (2)   wasn't   were   weren't

This is a picture of my grandma with my dad and his little brother. In the picture, they **1** _____ very young. My dad **2** _____ two years old. His brother **3** _____ one. Now they **4** _____ almost 50 years old! It **5** _____ summer in the picture. It was winter. My dad and his brother were usually happy children. But in this picture they **6** _____ happy at all! My grandma was also young in that picture. She **7** _____ old now, but still beautiful!

# 7 Find an old picture of your family. Show the picture to the class and talk about it.

This is a picture of me and my sister. We were at my birthday party …

# Language lab 2

**THERE WAS / THERE WERE**

*I will compare then and now.*

## 1 Read. Circle T (True) or F (False).

Yesterday I visited the museum. There were many fossils of fish. There wasn't a fossil of an ammonite, but I have a book with pictures of ammonites. They were like snails!

There weren't many people in the museum and it was quiet. There was a dinosaur skeleton and it was so big! There weren't any mammoths.

1   There was only one fossil of a fish at the museum.      T / F
2   There weren't any ammonite fossils at the museum.   T / F
3   There were a lot of people at the museum.      T / F
4   There wasn't a dinosaur skeleton at the museum.      T / F

## 2 Circle the correct word.

1   There **weren't** / **aren't** dinosaurs in the Ice Age.

2   There **were** / **are** a lot of children at the museum today.

3   There **wasn't** / **isn't** a mammoth in the book we read yesterday.

4   There **was** / **is** a fossil of a plant in our classroom today.

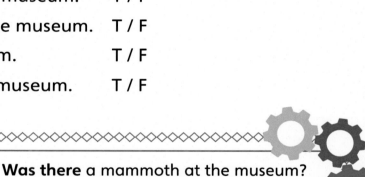

**Was there** a mammoth at the museum?
Yes, **there was.** / No, **there wasn't.**

**Were there** fossils at the museum?
Yes, **there were.** / No, **there weren't.**

## 3 Read and complete with the correct form of there was or there were.

1   _____ many saber tooth tigers in the Ice Age?

2   _____ a short-faced bear in the science book.

3   _____ any dinosaurs in the Ice Age. They lived in the Jurassic period.

# 3 Celebrations!

## 1  Watch. Which festival is more colorful than the Carnival in Rio de Janeiro? Check ☑.

1  Yi Peng Lantern Festival ☐

2  Thanksgiving Day Parade ☐

3  Castle Town Festival Parade ☐

## 2 ▷ Read and match. Watch to check.

1  Yi Peng Lantern Festival is ●

2  The Carnival in Rio de Janeiro is more ●

3  The Thanksgiving Day Parade looks more ●

4  The Castle Town Festival Parade is ●

● a  boring than the Carnival.

● b  better than the other festivals.

● c  quieter than other festivals.

● d  colorful and exciting than the festival in Thailand.

## 3 Look, read, and crack the code.

### CODE CRACKER ⚙⚙

| | | |
|---|---|---|
| costume: | colorful ✓✓✓ | interesting ✓✓ |
| book: | colorful ✓✓ | interesting ✓✓✓ |
| cake: | colorful ✓ | interesting ✗ |

1  X is more colorful than Y.

2  Z is more colorful than X.

3  Z is more colorful than Y.

4  Z is more interesting than Y.

5  X is more interesting than Z.

6  X is more interesting than Y.

X = _____    Y = _____    Z = _____

# Language lab 1

IT'S MORE ...

> I will learn to compare events.

## 1 Look at the picture and read. Choose the best title. Write.

1 A noisy carnival in Venice, Italy

2 Colorful costumes in Venice, Italy

3 Boring masks in Venice, Italy

● ● ●

_____

Hello! My name's Marco. This is a picture from the Carnival in Venice. People wear interesting clothes and big masks at the Carnival. They're more beautiful than masks from other festivals. The costumes are more colorful than the clothes we wear every day!

The Carnival in Venice is quieter than other carnivals. People walk around and look at costumes. I'm sure the Carnival in Rio de Janeiro is noisier!

This year my mom and my aunt were at the Carnival. My mom's mask was bigger and better than my aunt's. But her dress was worse than my aunt's. It wasn't very colorful.

## 2 Read again. Answer the questions. Check ☑.

1 Which carnival is quieter?

a the Carnival in Venice ☐

b the Carnival in Rio de Janeiro ☐

2 Whose dress was worse?

a his aunt's dress ☐

b his mom's dress ☐

---

Ben's costume is **good**. Mark's costume is **better than** Ben's.

Your mask is **big**. My mask is **bigger than** yours.

The white dress is **bad**. The black dress is **worse than** the white dress.

The Carnival in Venice is **exciting**. The Carnival in Rio **is more exciting than** the Carnival in Venice.

---

## 3 Read again. Underline the sentences that compare the carnivals, the masks, or the clothes.

# 4 Circle the different word.

1  better  happy  noisier       2  more exciting  colorful  worse
3  nicer  more interesting  tasty   4  hungry  happier  more boring

# 5 What's missing? Read and write.

1  The Carnival in Venice is more colorful _____ other carnivals around the world.

2  My mask is better _____ my sister's mask.

# 6 Complete the sentences with the correct form of the describing words.

1  The Carnival in Rio de Janeiro is _____ (noisy) than the Carnival in Venice.

2  The festival this year is _____ (good) than last year's festival.

3  The food at the party was _____ (bad) than the food at the restaurant.

4  The mask at this store is _____ (colorful) than the mask in the other store.

5  I think this movie is _____ (boring) than the book.

# 7 Look at the pictures. Work with a partner. Compare.

> Carnival – quiet   boat – colorful   boat – long   mask – short
> Carnival – interesting   Dragon Boat Festival – exciting

Carnival in Venice

Dragon Boat Festival

The boat is more colorful than the mask!

The Dragon Boat Festival is noisier than the Carnival ...

# Language lab 2

BEST, WORST, MOST EXCITING ...

> *I will learn to compare things using -est / most.*

## 1 Read. Which festival is the noisiest of all? Check ☑ the picture.

Carnival

Samba Festival

Dragon Boat Festival

Look at my photos! There are two Carnival masks, some samba drums, and a boat. The Samba Festival is the noisiest of all the festivals. The drums play all day. The Dragon Boat Festival is the most colorful of all. The most beautiful festival is the Carnival. The costumes are the most interesting thing of all.

The boat is **big**. The boat is **bigger** than the mask. The boat is **the biggest** thing at the Festival!

The Dragon Boat Festival is **exciting**. It is **more exciting** than the parade. The Dragon Boat Festival is **the most exciting** festival I know.

**Watch out!**

good → better → the best

bad → worse → the worst

## 2 Circle the correct word.

1 The parade is ( noisier / the noisiest ) event in our town.

2 Your dress is ( more colorful / the most colorful ) than my dress.

3 This band plays ( worse / the worst ) music of all the bands at the festival.

## 3 Put the words in order. Write.

1 the most   colorful   Your kite   of all   is   kite

_____ .

2 best   Pedro's party   was   the   party   of all

_____ .

# 4 Blast off!

**1** 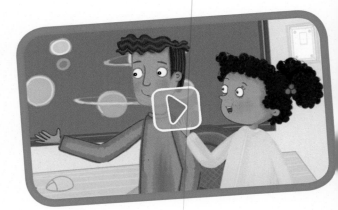 **Watch. Why is Chris Hadfield famous? Underline.**

1  He traveled to space many times.

2  He visited the Russian space station, Mir.

3  He played a musical instrument in space.

**2** **Complete with the past form of the words. Watch to check.**

> play   study   visit   walk

1  Chris Hadfield _____ the International Space Station.

2  Chris Hadfield _____ in space.

3  Chris Hadfield _____ gravity.

4  Chris Hadfield _____ the guitar in space.

**3** **Look at the events of Chris Hadfield's life. Underline the odd one out in each category.**

## CODE CRACKER

| Life on Earth | Life in Space |
|---|---|
| • watched the Apollo 11 Moon landing on TV | • studied at the Royal Military College |
| • joined the Canadian Space Agency in 1992 | • visited the ISS in 2001 |
| • visited the space station Mir | • played the guitar in space |

# Language lab 1

I will learn to talk about the past using -ed.

HE / SHE _____ ED.

## 1 Read Gary's email. Where was he yesterday? Check ☑.

1  on Earth ☐       2  on the Moon ☐       3  on the ISS ☐

Dear Grandma and Grandpa,

Hello from science camp! It's great!

Yesterday there was a guest at the camp. It was an astronaut. She talked about her work and her space missions. Last year she traveled to the ISS. Can you imagine that?! She didn't land on the Moon, but she traveled on a rocket and walked in space. She showed us some pictures. The Earth looked so small and beautiful from the space station.

I want to learn more about space and be an astronaut, too. I want to travel to space one day!

Love,

Gary

## 2 Read again. Circle T (True) or F (False).

1  Gary visited a space station.     T / F

2  The astronaut traveled on a rocket.     T / F

3  The astronaut landed on the Moon.     T / F

4  Gary wants to be an astronaut.   T / F

**Present**

I walk on the Moon every day.

She travels in space.

We don't launch rockets.

**Past**

I walk**ed** on the Moon yesterday.

She travel**ed** in space yesterday.

We **didn't** launch rockets yesterday.

## 3 Read again. Underline the action words that end in -ed.

19

## 4 Circle the correct word.

1  I walk / walked on the Moon yesterday.

2  They floated / float in space yesterday.

3  We don't launch / didn't launch the rocket yesterday.

4  The astronaut doesn't play / didn't play the guitar in space yesterday.

## 5 What's different? Read and complete the sentences with the words.

> walk   walked

Yesterday we _____ in space. We didn't _____ on the Moon.

## 6 Read. Complete the text with the correct form of the words.

> land   play   talk   walk   watch

I didn't **1** _____ television yesterday. I listened to a story on my computer about a rocket that traveled in space. The astronaut **2** _____ to the scientists on Earth about what he liked on another planet, Mars. He liked its color. It was very red! He didn't **3** _____ the guitar on Mars. He **4** _____ on the Moon after that. He **5** _____ for a few minutes on the Moon and then he traveled back to Earth.

# Language lab 2

DID HE / SHE ...?

## 1 Read. Did Hannah like her visit to the Space Museum? Check ☑.

yes ☐    no ☐

Hey, Hannah. When did you visit the Space Museum?

I visited the museum yesterday.

Did you enjoy it?

Yes, I did. I learned so many things!

What did you like?

I liked the pictures of the rockets.

Did you like the movie about Mars?

No, I didn't. We watched it at the end of our visit and I was tired!

Who did you see in the museum?

A scientist. He talked about how big Earth is. It's a lot smaller than the Sun!

How long did you stay at the museum?

We stayed for three hours.

## 2 Read and match.

1 What did Hannah like? ●

2 Did Hannah like the movie about Mars? ●

3 Who did Hannah see in the museum? ●

● a   No, she didn't.

● b   A scientist who talked about Earth.

● c   the pictures of the rockets

## 3 Circle the correct word.

1 What / Who / Where did you travel last year?

2 Why / Who / When did you watch on TV?

3 How / What / Where did you come to school today?

Did she visit her friends?
Yes, she did. / No, she didn't.

When did they start the class?
They started the class at eight o'clock.

## 4  Work with a partner. Ask and answer the questions in 3.

# 5 | Vacation time!

## 1  Watch. Choose the correct label for the picture. Check ☑.

1  Ellie had sand in her sandwiches. ☐

2  Ellie had a picnic on the beach. ☐

3  Ellie bought some ice cream. ☐

## 2 ▷ Read and match. Watch to check.

1  Ellie sat ●

2  They stayed ●

3  Ellie's brother bought ●

4  A crab bit ●

● a  Nadir.

● b  ice cream for breakfast.

● c  at a campsite.

● d  on the beach.

🇬🇧 **British**
holiday

🇺🇸 **American**
vacation

## 3 Look at the events. Were they good or bad? Sort them. Can you change one bad event to be good? Write.

## ||| CODE CRACKER ⚙⚙

A crab bit me.   I had picnics on the beach.   I got sand in my sandwiches. I swam in the ocean.   I was sea sick.

| 😃 | 🙁 |
|---|---|
| _____ | _____ |
| _____ | _____ |

_____

# Language lab 1

**I / YOU / HE / SHE / WE / THEY ...**

*I will learn to talk about what I / he / she / they did in the past.*

## 1 Look at the picture and read. What did David do last Saturday? Check ☑.

1 He swam in the sea. ☐
2 He went on vacation. ☐
3 He saw dolphins on his school trip. ☐
4 He read stories about animals. ☐

---

### Our boat trip *by David Jones*

Last Saturday, we went on a boat trip with my class. It was nice and quiet, when one of my classmates said "Look!" Three dolphins swam close to us and one of them jumped in the air. It was so cool!

When the boat trip was over, we went to a park and we ate our sandwiches. We played and ran around and it was so much fun. Then we bought ice cream and our teacher read us a story about a dolphin that swam around the world.

Then we got the bus and we sang songs all the way back home. It was such a great trip!

---

## 2 Read again. Circle T (True) or F (False).

1 David went on a boat trip. T / F
2 David was sea sick. T / F
3 Three dolphins swam near the boat. T / F
4 David and his classmates ate sandwiches in a park. T / F

> I **ate** sandwiches in the park last Saturday.
>
> I **didn't eat** sandwiches in the park last Sunday.
>
> She **swam** in the ocean yesterday.
>
> She **didn't see** any dolphins.

## 3 Read again. Underline the past forms of the action words.

## 4 Circle the correct word.

1  My brother ( see ) / ( saw ) five dolphins yesterday!

2  I ( did ) / ( do ) my homework late last night.

3  My dad ( buy ) / ( bought ) me a skateboard three days ago.

4  I ( swam ) / ( swim ) a lot on my last vacation.

## 5 Which time expressions can you normally use in the past? Circle.

yesterday

last month

last year

two weeks ago

always

every day

in 2017

on Saturdays

now

## 6 Complete the sentences with the words.

ago   ate   didn't swim   last   yesterday

1  Did you go on a school trip _____ week?

2  I didn't write many words in my book

   _____ .

3  I _____ yesterday. I didn't have my swimsuit!

4  She ran 20 kilometers three months _____.

5  He _____ all the ice cream! I didn't eat any.

## 7 Tell your partner about your favorite vacation.

When I was six years old I went on vacation …

# Language lab 2

DID YOU / HE / SHE ...?

## 1 Read. What did Eric see in the ocean? Underline.

**Tim:** Hey, Eric. How was your weekend? What did you do?

**Eric:** Hi, Tim. It was great! I went to the beach with my dad.

**Tim:** Really? I was there, too! When did you go?

**Eric:** We were there at ten o'clock on Saturday. Who did you go with?

**Tim:** I went with my big brother on Sunday evening. We sat on the beach and then we swam. What did you do?

**Eric:** First, we ran on the beach. Then we saw a whale. Did you see any?

**Tim:** No, we didn't. We only saw crabs and fish!

**Did** you **swim** in the ocean?

Yes, I did. / No, I didn't.

Where **did** she **go** camping?

**Remember!**

when → time

who → person

what → thing

why → reason

how → the way to do something

## 2 Read again and circle.

1 When did Eric go to the beach?

   a on Sunday        b on Saturday

2 Who did Tim go to the beach with?

   a his brother       b his dad

3 What did Tim see on the beach?

   a He saw fish and crabs.    b He saw fish and whales.

## 3 Complete the dialog with the words.

how   what   when   where   who

**Joanna:** 1 _____ animals did you see on your vacation?

**Marta:** I saw dolphins and whales. And I saw some crabs.

**Joanna:** That's great! 2 _____ did you stay? 3 _____ did you go with?

**Marta:** We stayed at a campsite by the sea. I went with my mom, dad, and sister.

**Joanna:** And 4 _____ did you come back? 5 _____ did you travel?

**Marta:** We came back three days ago. We traveled by boat.

# Let's shop!

**1** 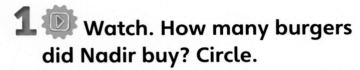 **Watch. How many burgers did Nadir buy? Circle.**

20    30

**2** **Complete the sentences with these words. Watch to check.**

some   many   much   any

1  Do you have _____ bread rolls?

2  How _____ bread rolls do you think, Ellie?

3  How _____ is that big chocolate cake?

4  What about _____ healthy stuff, too?

| 🇬🇧 British |
| --- |
| have got |
| 🇺🇸 American |
| have |

**3** **Read the dialog. Follow the pattern to write a new dialog. Use some of the words from the box.**

## CODE CRACKER

apples   bakery   cakes
carrots   cook   eight   oranges
run   fourteen   twenty-five

A:  Do you have any <u>bread rolls</u>?

B:  Yes, of course. How many would you like?

A:  I'd like <u>30</u> bread rolls, please.

_____

_____

_____

# Language lab 1

THERE IS / ARE A / SOME ...

## 1 Read the note. What does Oscar's mom want? Check ☑ .

1   She wants to work late.

2   She wants to go to the store.

3   She wants help with the picnic shopping.

Hi, kids!

I'm working late tonight. Can you please go together to the store and buy the things on this list for our picnic? There is some money on the table.

- We need some apples and some oranges. There aren't any at home.
- I think there's some cheese. Please don't buy any more.
- We need some chips. You can buy your favorite kind!
- There isn't any juice. Please buy some.
- Can you buy some pasta, too? I want to make a pasta salad.
- And we also need a cake!

That's all! You can get some ice cream, too. Oscar, be good and listen to your sister. See you later tonight!

Love,

Mom

## 2 Read again. Circle T (True) or F (False).

1   There are many apples
    at Oscar's home.          T / F

2   There is some cheese
    at Oscar's home.          T / F

3   There isn't any juice
    for the picnic.           T / F

I have **some** rice and **some** pasta.

I don't have **any** bread.

Can you buy **a** mango and **an** apple?

Are there **any** bananas in the basket?

**3** Read the text on page 27 again. Underline the sentences with *some* in blue and *any* in red.

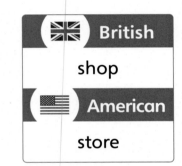

> **Count nouns**
> = things you can count –
> one apple, two apples ☑
> **Non-count nouns**
> = things you can't count –
> one cheese, two cheeses ☒

**4** Circle the correct word.

1 There isn't ( some / any ) water in the kitchen.
2 There are ( some / any ) oranges at the store.
3 There is ( some / any ) milk in my glass.
4 There aren't ( some / any ) carrots in the bag.

**5** Complete the sentences with a/an, some, or any.

1 There is _____ carrot on the table.
2 We don't have _____ cheese.
3 Is there _____ apple in your bag?
4 There is _____ rice in the kitchen.
5 There isn't _____ pasta at the store.
6 Do you want _____ sugar in your tea?

> 🇬🇧 British
> shop
> 🇺🇸 American
> store

**6** 🌐 What's in your fridge? Draw. Ask and answer with a partner.

Are there any carrots?

Yes, there are some carrots.

# Language lab 2

HOW MUCH / MANY ...?

I will learn to ask about amount using **How much ...?**

## 1 Read. How many pizzas does Elena need? Check ☑.

some ☐     a bag ☐     three ☐     four ☐

---

**Elena:** What do we need for my birthday party, Mom?

**Mom:** Let's see. We don't have much salad. We need one bag.

**Elena:** How many pizzas can we have?

**Mom:** Well, you have three friends coming to your party. Let's get three pizzas!

**Elena:** How much fruit do we need?

**Mom:** We don't need any. We have a lot of fruit.

**Elena:** How many bread rolls should we get?

**Mom:** Let's get one for all of us!

**Elena:** So, four? One for each of us at the party?

**Mom:** No, five. I want one, too!

## 2 Read again. Answer the questions.

1   How much salad do they need?          _____

2   How much fruit do they have?          _____

3   How many bread rolls do they need?    _____

## 3 Circle the correct words.

1   How  much / many  pears do you have?

2   I don't like  much / many  salt on my food.

3   How  much / a lot of  rice do you want?

4   I have  a lot of / many  fruit in my lunchbox.

**How many** apples do we need?

We don't need **many** apples.

**How much** rice do we need?

We don't need **much** rice.

We need **a lot of / lots of** apples / rice.

# 7 Eco Warriors!

**1** ▶ **Watch. What is the Eco Warrior Challenge? Check ☑ .**

a   a competition to protect the planet ☐

b   a competition to plant flowers ☐

c   a competition to save plastic bottles ☐

**2** ▶ **Complete with the correct form of be going to. Watch to check.**

1   I _____ plant some plants.

2   Where _____ you _____ plant them?

3   What _____ Yara _____ do for the competition?

4   She _____ recycle trash.

**3 Look at what Ellie is going to do and the result. Put the events in the right order.**

## CODE CRACKER

get more bees and butterflies    plant flowers
put flowers around the clubhouse    use old plastic bottles as pots

**1** [        ]  →  **2** [        ]  →  **3** [        ]

**4** [        ]

**RESULT:** help the planet  ←

# Language lab 1

WHAT ARE YOU GOING TO DO?

> I will learn to talk about the future using **going to**.

## 1 Read the messages. Choose the best sentence. Check ☑.

a   Dan and Emily are going to do something for the Save the Planet Weekend. ☐

b   Dan and Emily are going to visit a wildlife park with their class. ☐

Dear Dan,

The Save the Planet Weekend is so cool! I'm going to clean up trash in the park.

We're going to meet in the park on Saturday and we're going to start with the plastic trash. Then, I'm going to pick up the glass bottles. We're going to recycle them all.

What are you going to do?

Bye,

Emily

Hi, Emily!

I'm also happy about the Save the Planet Weekend. I'm going to go to the park on Sunday.

We're going to make posters about how to save wildlife. I'm going to draw tigers! Our group is going to meet on Sunday at 11. Our teacher is going to draw a poster of our planet!

See you at school,

Dan

## 2 Who are the sentences about? Write E (Emily) or D (Dan).

1   I'm going to go to the park on Sunday. _____

2   I'm going to clean up trash in the park. _____

3   I'm going to pick up the glass bottles. _____

4   I'm going to draw tigers! _____

## 3 Read again. Underline the sentences with going to.

What **are** you **going to** do?

We're **going to** reduce trash.

We **aren't going to** waste paper.

# 4 Circle the correct word.

1   It's so dirty in the school yard. I ( am going / am not going ) to pick up trash.

2   He's really happy, he ( 's going to / 's not going ) go to the zoo.

3   What ( are you / you are ) going to do this weekend?

4   We need new flower pots. We ( are to / are going to ) use old plastic bottles.

5   Please hurry up, we ( 're going to / 'm going to ) be late.

# 5 Complete the sentences with the words.

> are going to   going   is going to   isn't going   they're going

1   My sister _____ to go to school tomorrow. She's sick.

2   Jim _____ put paper and glass bottles in the recycling bin.

3   _____ to do their homework before they go to the park.

4   Is your brother _____ to visit the zoo next week?

5   My friends _____ visit me next week. I'm so happy!

# 6 Put the words in order to make questions.

1   to   plastic bottles   they   reuse   going   are

   _Are they going to reuse plastic bottles?_

2   school   go   to   to   he   is   tomorrow   going

   _____ ?

3   go   they   to   by bus   are   going

   _____ ?

4   to   recycle   going   are   you   glass bottles

   _____ ?

5   she   watch   going   a   movie   to   is

   _____ ?

# 7 💬 Now change the questions in 6 and ask and answer with a partner.

> Are **you** going to reuse plastic bottles?

# Language lab 2

I WANT / WOULD LIKE TO ...

> I will learn to talk about wants using **I want / would like to ...**

## 1 Read. What does Mia's teacher want to do? Check ☑.

reuse paper ☐    make a zoo ☐    save wildlife ☐

Hi, I'm Mia and I'm eight years old. These are my dreams!

Our planet is in danger and I want to protect it. My friends at school want to save wildlife, too! We would like to live in a clean environment. We don't want to throw away so much trash. We would like to reuse and recycle more!

My sister wants to plant trees all over the city. My dad would like to compost the food we throw out. My mom wants to make a wildlife zoo!

I don't want to play in dirty parks or see trash on the streets. My teacher doesn't want to throw away paper. She would like to reuse it!

I think we can all do many things to protect and save our planet. Let's try!

## 2 Read again. Match.

1  My dad would •          • a   to reuse more.
2  My mom wants •          • b   like to compost food.
3  I don't want •          • c   to make a wildlife zoo.
4  We would like •          • d   to play in dirty parks.

## 3 Circle the correct words.

1  I want ( recycle / to recycle ) trash at home.

2  We ( don't want / don't want to ) leave trash on the street.

3  She ( would like to / would like ) reuse paper and glass.

> I **want to** recycle more trash.
>
> She **doesn't want to** waste water.
>
> They **would like to** clean the park.

**I'd like to** = I would like to

# 8 Let's work!

**1** ▷ **Watch. What does Nadir ask Ellie to do? Check ☑ .**

a help him design something on the computer ☐

b help him clean the rabbits' cage ☐

c help him with his homework ☐

**2** ▷ **Read and complete with the correct form of the words. Watch to check.**

> clean   do (2)   play

1 I don't always like _____ homework.

2 I enjoy _____ design projects.

3 I love _____ with the rabbits.

4 I don't like _____ out their cage.

**3** ▷ **Read and correct the mistakes. Watch to check.**

## CODE CRACKER ⚙️⚙️

1 I enjoy cleaning out design projects.

2 I don't like coding and programming.

3 I don't like doing challenging things.

4 I hate doing the rabbits' cage.

5 I hate feeding the rabbits.

# Language lab 1

I LIKE / DON'T LIKE …

I will learn to talk about my preferences using **I like / don't like …**

**1** **Read the text. What is Lisa's dream job? Check ☑ .**

a doctor ☐   b nurse ☐

● ● ●

Hi Angela,

I'm a student at Brent School. I'm happy that you're going to visit our school in October. I'm writing to tell you about my dream job.

I love helping people. I like studying very much and I love learning about the human body. I would like to be a doctor.

I enjoy working with other people. I think that working with nurses and other doctors can be nice. But I don't like staying up in the night. I think that working at night is difficult and getting up early on the weekend isn't easy, too!

What about you? Do you like helping people?

See you in October!

Lisa

**2** **Read again. Circle T (True) or F (False).**

1 Lisa doesn't like helping people.   T / F
2 Lisa likes learning.   T / F
3 Lisa enjoys working with others.   T / F
4 Lisa likes getting up early.   T / F

I **like** study**ing**.
You **enjoy** read**ing**.
He **loves** help**ing** people.

They **don't enjoy** danc**ing**.

**Does** she **like** watch**ing** TV?
Yes, she does. / No, she doesn't.

**3** **Read again. Underline the activities Lisa likes in green, loves in blue, or enjoys in red.**

## 4 Circle the correct word.

1   I like (play) / playing  basketball.

2   Amy (love reading) / loves reading  books.

3   Do you enjoy (listening) / listens  to music?

4   We (not) / don't like  watching TV.

5   Do you like riding a bike? No, (I do) / I don't .

## 5 ⚙ What is missing? Read and complete the sentences.

I like play _____ the piano and Mary loves play _____ the piano.
Tony doesn't like watch _____ TV.

## 6 💬 Use the correct form of the words to ask and answer questions.

> enjoy   hate   like   love
> not enjoy   not like

> cook food   do karate   play the violin
> play video games   read books   ride a bike

> Do you enjoy reading books?

> Yes, I love reading books!

## 7 ✴ Draw the activity you love from 6! Show it to another partner to guess.

> Do you love doing karate?

> No, sorry. Try again!

# Language lab 2

WHY DO / ARE YOU ...

> I will learn to ask and answer questions using **Why** and **Because**.

## 1 Read. Why does Diego want to be a nurse? Check ☑.

Because he likes houses. ☐          Because he likes cars. ☐

Because he likes computers. ☐      Because he likes helping people. ☐

**Teacher:** Today we are talking about jobs. What is your favorite job and why?

**Paola:** I want to be an architect because I like houses and I like drawing.

**Teacher:** What about you, Diego?

**Diego:** I want to be a nurse because I like helping people.

**Teacher:** And Kevin? What job do you want to do?

**Kevin:** I want to be a mechanic because I like cars.

**Teacher:** OK. And you, Mary? What job do you like?

**Mary:** I love computer programming.

**Teacher:** Why do you want to be a computer programmer?

**Mary:** Because you can do many useful things with computers.

## 2 Read again. Match.

1 Why does Paola want to be an architect? ●—

2 Why does Kevin want to be a mechanic? ●—

3 Why does Mary want to be a computer programmer? ●—

●  a  Because she can do many useful things with computers.

●  b  Because she likes houses.

●  c  Because he likes cars.

**Why** do you like computer programming? **Because** it's interesting.

## 3 Read the answers. Write the questions.

1 _____ ?

I want to be a vet because I like animals.

2 _____ ?

We aren't riding our bikes because it's raining.

# Extra Grammar 1

NEED + INFINITIVE

> I will talk about my duties using **need**.

## 1 Read. What do Mark and his parents need to do on Saturdays? Check ☑.

**a** They need to clean. ☐      **b** They need to visit family. ☐

My name is Mark. You can see me in the photo. I'm cleaning my room. It's Saturday morning.

We all have different jobs on Saturdays. First, I need to pick up all my clothes. Then I need to clean my room. My mom doesn't need to help me. My dad needs to wash the plates. He needs to take out the trash, too. We get really tired. I'm glad that I don't need to clean every day.

wash the plates

After we finish, we always rest. We don't need to do any more jobs for the rest of the day.

When do you need to clean?

## 2 Read again and match.

1 I don't need to ●          ● **a** take out the trash.

2 Dad needs to ●            ● **b** help me.

3 First, I need to ●         ● **c** clean every day.

4 My mom doesn't need to ●  ● **d** pick up all my clothes.

## 3 Read again. Underline all the sentences with need to.

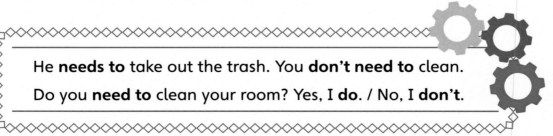

He **needs to** take out the trash. You **don't need to** clean.

Do you **need to** clean your room? Yes, I **do**. / No, I **don't**.

38

## 4 Circle the correct word.

1  My dad ( needs to ) / ( need to ) clean the kitchen.

2  On weekends we ( need to ) / ( don't need to ) go to school.

3  My mom ( need to ) / ( needs to ) work in the morning.

4  The students in my class ( needs to ) / ( need to ) work hard.

5  Do you ( need to ) / ( needs to ) do homework every day?

## 5 Read the sentences and complete the rules.

a  I need to do my homework.

b  He needs to tidy up his room.

c  We don't need to go to school.

d  She doesn't need to cook.

We use *needs* with 1 _____
and *need* with 2 _____ .

We add 3 _____ or
4 _____ to make negative sentences.

## 6 Put the words in order. Write three more sentences with need to that are true for you.

1  ( needs ) ( the ) ( plates ) ( to ) ( wash ) ( He )

_____ .

2  ( I ) ( don't ) ( pick up ) ( to ) ( need ) ( clothes ) ( my )

_____ .

3  ( needs ) ( to ) ( My ) ( sister ) ( do her homework )

_____ .

4  _____ .

5  _____ .

6  _____ .

# Extra Grammar 2

AND, BUT, BECAUSE, SO

> I will link ideas using **and**, **but**, **because**, **so**.

**1** **Read. How old was Usain Bolt when he became a professional runner? Check ☑.**

a fourteen ☐  b twelve ☐  c eighteen ☐  d eight ☐

**Usain Bolt is one of the fastest people on Earth. Usain was born in Jamaica in 1986. He loved sports and always played a lot of soccer. He was a very good runner, too, so he chose to work hard on running.**

When he was twelve, he was the fastest runner at school. His father said he was fast because he ate a lot of potatoes! When he was fifteen, he went to the World Athletics Championships. He won the 200-meter race in a record time.

Usain became a professional runner when he was eighteen. In 2005, he went to another World Championships. He got into the finals, but he finished last! Then, at the Beijing Olympic Games in 2008, he won a gold medal in the 100 meters in a record time of 9.89 seconds.

In 2016 at the Rio Olympics in Brazil, Usain won gold in the 100 meters again! He has eight Olympic gold medals.

**2** **Read and circle T (True) or F (False).**

1 Usain was a good soccer player, but not a good runner.  T / F

2 Usain's father said that eating potatoes made Usain fast.  T / F

3 Usain didn't go to the World Championships.  T / F

> She did gymnastics **and** she was good at it.
>
> You were the fastest runner **because** you worked hard.
>
> They worked hard, **so** they were the fastest runners.
>
> They worked hard, **but** they weren't the fastest runners.

**3** Read the text on page 40 again. Underline the sentences with and, because, so, and but.

**4** Read and match.

1  I went to the store, •           • a  because we studied a lot.
2  We got a good grade •          • b  so I came first.
3  She didn't sleep well, •        • c  but it was closed.
4  I ran the fastest, •            • d  so she didn't feel well in the morning.

**5** Read and circle a or b.

1  I like going to school _____ I learn many things every day.
   a  because                      b  but
2  On Saturday, I tidy up my room _____ play with my friends.
   a  and                          b  but
3  I didn't do my homework, _____ I need to do it now.
   a  because                      b  so

**6** Complete the sentences with and, but, so, or because.

1  I didn't invite Kate to my party, _____ she wasn't happy.
2  My brother is the best student in the school _____ he studies a lot.
3  On Thursday evenings we go swimming _____ then watch a movie.
4  He is very fast, _____ he didn't come first.

**7** Say a sentence for your partner to complete. Take turns and use and, because, but, so.

I like dancing because …

… I like music.

I came to your house, but …

… you weren't there.

# Extra Grammar 3

IF YOU COME IN APRIL, IT RAINS.

> I will learn to use the Zero Conditional.

**1** Read. If you love walking, when is the best time to visit the park? Underline.

## Yosemite National Park is beautiful in all seasons!

If you like snow and winter sports, then the best time to visit the park is **winter**! If you don't have winter boots, you can find some at one of our centers!

**Spring** is the perfect season if you like walking by the river! Wear warm clothes and a raincoat if you want to walk in the mountains. The weather changes quickly! If you come in April, it usually rains or snows.

**Summer** is the time to come if you want to take pictures of all the wild flowers in the park! There are many tourists. If you don't want to wait long at the entrance, you need to be in the park early.

If you visit the park in **fall**, Yosemite Park's trees are full of beautiful colors. Their colors are amazing when the weather is dry, and the temperatures don't go below 0°C. This time is perfect for riding a bike, too.

**2** Read again. Circle T (True) or F (False).

1   You can get winter boots at the park.          T / F
2   In Yosemite, it usually rains or snows in June.  T / F
3   If you like flowers, visit Yosemite in fall.      T / F

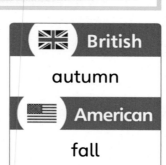

🇬🇧 British
autumn

🇺🇸 American
fall

**3** Read the text on page 42 again. Underline the sentences with **if**.

**4** Circle the correct word.

Winter **is** the best time to visit if you **like** snow.

If you **come** in April, it **rains** or **snows**.

If you **don't want** to wait long, you **need** to come early.

1 If you are sick, you ( aren't feeling ) / ( don't feel ) well.

2 The river ( freezes ) / ( is freezing ) if it's very cold.

3 I ( walk ) / ( walks ) to school if the weather is nice.

4 If people ( don't ) / ( doesn't ) eat, they get hungry.

**5** Complete the sentences with the correct form of the action words.

1 If it _____ (rain), I wear my rain boots.

2 Plants don't grow if you _____ (not/water) them.

3 If you freeze water, it _____ (turn) into ice.

4 If it _____ (be) dark, you don't see much.

5 If you _____ (not/sleep) well, you are tired.

6 People smile if they _____ (be) happy.

**6** Work with a partner. Choose and say.

rain/wear my raincoat    sunny/go for a walk
study a lot/do well at school    meet my friends/laugh a lot
help my mom/give me a hug

If it rains, …

… I wear my raincoat!

# Grammar Reference

## Unit 1

### Language lab 1

**Present Progressive:**

What *are you doing*?
*I'm riding* the bus with my friends.
*We're going* to school.

What*'s* he *doing*?
*He's drawing. He isn't reading*.

What *are they doing*?
*They're singing. They aren't acting*.

*Is she waving*?
Yes, *she is*.

*Are they drinking* juice?
No, *they aren't*.

### Language lab 2

**Present Progressive with adverbs of manner:**

I'm juggling *well*.
He's drawing *beautifully*.
They're singing *badly*.
We're going to school *quickly*.
We're not going to school *slowly*.

## Unit 2

### Language lab 1

**Simple Past of *be*:**

It *was* snowy last winter.
It *wasn't* warm.
We *were* in the yard.

*Was* it windy?
Yes, it *was*.

*Were* you tired?
No, we *weren't*.

### Language lab 2

***There was/There were*:**

*There was* a tree in the yard. *There wasn't* a path.
*There were* birds in the yard. *There weren't* any rabbits.

*Was there* a cat?
No, *there wasn't*.
*Were there* nuts on the table? Yes, *there were*.

# Unit 3

## Language lab 1

**Comparatives:**

The show is *more exciting* than the play.
The show is *noisier* than the play.
The play is *quieter* than the show.
The music at the play is *worse* than the music at the show.

## Language lab 2

**Superlatives:**

This is the *best* show ever!
It has the *biggest* and the *most colorful* stage in the world.
The magic tricks are the *most exciting* part of the show.
The people on stage wear the *funniest* clothes, but the music is the *worst* I've ever heard.

# Unit 4

## Language lab 1

**Simple Past with regular verbs:**

I *traveled* by train.
I *didn't travel* by airplane.
You *visited* your aunty.
You *didn't visit* your uncle.
He *studied* math yesterday.
He *didn't study* English.
She *worked* in the farm.
She *didn't work* in the café.
They *played* soccer.
They *didn't play* basketball.

## Language lab 2

**Simple Past with regular verbs:**

Where *did* you *travel* to?
I *traveled* to Mexico.

When *did* she *work* at the bakery?
She *worked* there on Saturday.

Who *did* he *study* with?
He *studied* with his friend.

*Did* you *swim* in the river?
No, I *didn't*.

*Did* she *walk* to the store?
Yes, she *did*.

# Grammar Reference

## Unit 5

### Language lab 1

**Simple Past with irregular verbs:**

I *went* to the cafe and
I *bought* some juice.
You *did* your homework.
He *sat* on the chair.
He *didn't sit* on the table.
She *saw* her friend.
She *didn't see* her teacher.
We *had* three pencils.
We *didn't have* an eraser.
They *ate* all the cookies.
They *didn't eat* all the salad.

### Language lab 2

**Simple Past with irregular verbs:**

*Did* you *buy* some water?
No, I *didn't*.

Where *did* she *do* her homework?
She *did* her homework in the library.

How many pencils *did* they *have*?
They *had* three pencils.

What *did* they *eat*?
They *ate* cookies.

## Unit 6

### Language lab 1

**Countable and uncountable nouns:**

There is *a* kite in the toy store.
There is *an* astronaut in
the toy store.
There is *some* bread in
the bakery.
There are *some* cakes in
the cafe.
There isn't *any* cheese in
the market.

### Language lab 2

**Countable and uncountable nouns:**

There's *a lot of* bread in the bakery.
There are *lots of* balls in the toy store.
There isn't *much* pizza left.
There aren't *many* cookies in the jar.

How *much* money does the kite cost? $10
How *many* cakes are there? There are
three cakes.

# Unit 7

## Language lab 1

***Going to* to talk about the future:**

What are you *going to* do tomorrow?
I'm *going to* go to the beach with my family.
Mom's *going to* relax. She *isn't going to* cook.
My brothers are *going to* go surfing.
I'm *not going to* go surfing.

## Language lab 2

**Infinitives of purpose: *want to* and *would like to*:**

I *want to* go on a boat trip. I'*d like to* see a dolphin. I *don't want to* see a shark.
I *wouldn't like to* see its teeth!
My mom *wants to* have a picnic.
My dad *doesn't want to* have a picnic.
My brothers *want to* play soccer.
They *don't want to* play volleyball.

# Unit 8

## Language lab 1

**Like / enjoy / love:**

Do *you like doing* sports at school?
Yes, I do.
*I like doing* gymnastics.
*He enjoys studying* English.
*She loves going* to the museum. *She doesn't enjoy going* to the mall.
*We like going* to the playground.
*They love eating* carrots.
*They don't like swimming*.

## Language lab 2

***Why* and *Because*:**

*Why* do you like going to the playground?
*Because* I can have fun with my friends.

*Why* is he studying English?
*Because* he wants to travel.

*Why* does she like going to the museum?
*Because* she likes looking at fossils.

**Pearson Education Limited**
KAO TWO
KAO Park
Hockham Way
Harlow, Essex
CM17 9SR
England

and Associated Companies throughout the world.

english.com/englishcode

First published 2021
Second impression 2024

ISBN: 978-1-292-35453-8

Set in Heinemann Roman 13.5pt
Printed and bound by CPI Group (UK) Ltd, Croydon, CR0 4YY

**Image Credits:**

**123RF.com:** Andrea Izzotti 23, annunnal 27, Cathy Yeulet 33, Dmytro Zinkevych 32, Konrad Mostert 25, patl38241 35, ulisse 17; **Alamy Stock Photo:** ZUMA Press 40; **Getty Images:** Mima Foto/EyeEm 8, 18, 28; **Pearson Education Ltd:** Jon Barlow 8, 12, 24, 28, 36, 43, Jules Selmes 5, Studio 8 8; **Shutterstock.com:** 2xSamara.com 31, Alohaflaminggo 31, Alones 20, Andy Z 42, Anna Nahabed 9, Anna Photographer 8, 16, Belinka 38, Chen Min Chun 16, 17, Colin D. Young 42, DenisProduction.com 7, Dmitri Ma 29, Elzbieta Sekowska 12, Galyna Andrushko 42, Izabela23 15, Lukas Gojda 15, 17, 19, 29, 33, Naphat_Jorjee 37, Nic Neish 7, Olena Yakobchuk 19, Pakula Piotr 38, Pavel L Photo and Video 13, Pedro Maria 16, Phaitoon Sutunyawatchai 13, Pressmaster 5, Ramon Espelt Photography 18, 28, Richard Susanto 42, Robbi 9, 27, Sergey Novikov 5, 39, Shutterstock 5, 11, 24, Sonpichit Salangsing 21, timquo 24, 27, 34, 43, Val Thoermer 17, wavebreakmedia 36

**Animation screen shots**

Artwork by Lesley Danson/Bright Agency, production by Dardanele Studio

All other images © Pearson Education

Illustrated by Chiara Fiorentino/Astound US, pp. 4, 28; Lucy Semple/Bright Agency, pp. 44-45; Amy Wilcox/Lemonade Illustration, pp. 46-47.

**Cover Image:** *Front:* **Pearson Education Ltd:** Jon Barlow